SEEN:
Discovering the Freedom to Be Authentically You

An Eight-Week Guided Journey

By Lynne Farrell

Thy Name Publishing

SEEN: Discovering the Freedom to Be Authentically You;
An Eight-Week Guided Journey

Website: www.seenandbeloved.com

Publisher: Thy Name, Inc. (McLean, VA)
www.thy-name.com

Cover Images: Fiverr image with ChatGPT

ISBN: 978-1-7368128-9-1

CONTENTS

A Letter to the Participant

"Then you will experience for yourselves the truth, and the truth will free you." John 8:32 (MSG)

Dear Participant,

Thank you for choosing to take part in "SEEN: Discovering the Freedom to Be Authentically You." My heartfelt prayer is that during our time together, pondering God's Word and tuning in to His voice, you will be awakened through the Spirit to begin or continue in a lifelong, joyful journey of true freedom, life, and love. I have been studying Scripture with other women for several decades now, and I have never been disappointed in the treasures I discover. God sends His messages in trinkets and troves, in conviction and in reassurance, through His Holy pages and through the mouths of others. As a result, I have never been more certain of Who the Holy One is or more personally defined by His definitions of me. Small group Bible study, in so many ways, has been my lifeline.

The format of each small group using this study will vary slightly, depending on what length of time the group chooses to meet each week, but the basic format and structure will not change. There are eight sessions in total, and each one consists of a short video teaching from me accompanied by related questions to help guide the group's discussion. You will find that when used together, these tools can help position you to more fully receive essential truths about your identity and Jesus' character, while at the same time building an authentic community of friends you will come to know and trust with your unique, and sometimes painful, stories.

There is no required homework, but the best thing you can do to enhance this study is to pray and reflect on your own between group meetings. The "Digging Deeper" section at the end of each chapter is designed to enhance and solidify the truths that were introduced during small group, giving you suggestions for personal reflection and listening space, which will ultimately cultivate a deeper of relationship between you and Jesus. I encourage you to take the extra time to be with Him. You will not regret it!

In addition, I have included 10 ways to "Set the Seen" (Appendix 1) to help you learn to recognize when your heavenly Father is showing you the deep, abiding love He has for you. As I often say, "When you start to see Him seeing you with eyes of love, everything changes."

As His beloved and cherished daughter, joyfully receive every blessing that is yours in Christ!

You are Seen,

Lynne

<u>The Authentic Life</u>
by Lynne Farrell

I was created for life, life in the truest, life in the fullest, life in Christ.

I was created for abundance.

I was designed to be me, uniquely, fully, and with divine, Kingdom purpose.

I was designed on purpose.

I came alive in Jesus and have now been restored to my true self; no longer tied to the old way and the old me.

I was made alive in Christ Jesus.

My stories have the potential for God's redemption: to bring heaven to earth, to bring wholeness to others, and to supernaturally unite God's children, and I surrender them to Jesus for Him to use for His healing as He writes my new story for the world.

I have a new story.

I do not need to live in the shadows of shame or the confinement of unforgiveness. I am a daughter of the Most High King, and my Father adores me.

I am designated to be free.

He sees me, and His deepest desire is for me to see the way He looks at me, with wonder and with adoration and with full understanding. Nothing is hidden, and nothing in all the world could be more glorious.

I am His, and He is mine. This the greatest
of all truths.

This the essence of being SEEN.

SESSION 1

SEEN:

Fully Alive

SMALL-GROUP DISCUSSION QUESTIONS

1. Introduce yourself by sharing your name, where you live, and a single, positive word you would use to describe yourself.

2. Why did you join this study, and what do you hope to get out of it?

3. Where have you seen "masks" worn in our society? Why do you think they are so common?

4. Are you in agreement with Lynne that "transparency opens up transparency"? When have you seen this to be true?

5. Describe a time when you really felt seen by another person. Why do you think it stands out in your memory?

6. Have you ever shared your heart in a vulnerable way with others? Why did you feel you could be transparent? What was the result?

7. In what ways do you believe Jesus was "fully alive"? Do you believe He wants the same for you? Why, or why not?

DIGGING DEEPER

Below are some recommended questions and activities to use in your personal devotion time this week.

1. **Review** the group discussion questions (above), and record in your journal any of your answers or answers of other women in your group that were particularly meaningful to you.

2. **Pray** about how you might be changed by participating in this study. Do you sense any invitation from the Lord? Each week, practice opening your heart to what He wants to do.

3. **Read** Luke 4:18–19 where Jesus states His mission for leaving heaven and coming to earth. **Reflect** on why "freedom for the prisoners" and "liberty to the oppressed" (ESV) is part of that mission and what this might mean to you.

4. **Read** John 4:1–26, and imagine you are the woman Jesus meets at the well. **Reflect** on what you think Jesus meant when He talked about "living water" (v. 10) and how those who drink this will "never thirst" (v. 14).

5. **Ask the Lord** to reveal to you over the next week a memory of when your true self was seen by someone. **Thank Him** for that person and for their sincere interest in seeing the real you.

6. **Listen** to one of your favorite praise songs and practice resting in His presence.

7. **"Set the Seen"** by choosing to do an activity from Appendix 1. Record in your journal what the Holy Spirit reveals and how you feel knowing you are seen by God.

SESSION 2

SEEN:

Divine Offering

SMALL-GROUP DISCUSSION QUESTIONS

1. If you completed any of the "Digging Deeper" exercises during the week and you feel comfortable sharing, explain what you learned or experienced.

2. Read Genesis 16:1–13. How do think Hagar felt before and after she encounters "The One who sees me"?

3. Do you remember a time when you felt seen by God? Describe the details. What do you think He was trying to say to you in allowing you to sense this?

4. Are you able to identify a "thorny thread," a pervasive lie that has been threaded through your life? Do you know when it began? Do you think you still struggle with it now?

5. Do you ever remember feeling as though a Bible verse was true, yet it couldn't make it to your heart? Why do you think that happens?

6. Have you ever felt stuck in your faith journey? If yes, describe what helped you out. If you feel are in that place right now, consider sharing with your group.

7. What do you believe Jesus's promise to give us "life to the full" (John 10:10) includes? Do you feel like you are experiencing it in your life now?

DIGGING DEEPER

Below are some recommended questions and activities to use in your personal devotion time this week.

1. **Review** the group discussion questions (above), and record in your journal any of your answers or answers of other women in your group that were particularly meaningful to you.

2. **Pray** and ask the Holy Spirit to help you identify any lies that you know you have believed, perhaps most of your life. **Allow** Him to stir up desire in your heart for freedom from any "thorny thread" that may have resulted.

3. **Read** John 10:1–18. **Reflect** on what Jesus means when He calls Himself the Good Shepherd and what effect that has on you receiving "life to the full".

4. **Read** Mark 5:1–20. **Reflect** on the impact the demonic man's radically changed life might have had on the people of this town.

5. **Ask the Lord** to speak to you about the lies you have believed, the "thorny thread" that's been woven through your life story, or the way you've been attempting to get abundant life outside of His love. Ask Him to help you experience the truth, and **thank Him** ahead of His healing.

6. **Listen** to one of your favorite praise songs and practice resting in His presence.

7. **"Set the Seen"** by choosing to do an activity from Appendix 1. Record in your journal what the Holy Spirit reveals and how you feel knowing you are seen by God.

SESSION 3

SEEN:

Unmasked

SMALL-GROUP DISCUSSION QUESTIONS

1. If you completed any of the "Digging Deeper" exercises during the week and you feel comfortable sharing, explain what you learned or experienced.

2. Do you recognize any masks that you tend to put on? Why do you think you prefer disguises to your "true and beloved self"?

3. What is your reaction to the review of Jesus' victory and how He satisfies all our desires (see *Christ's Victory* chart on page 21)? Was this new information for you?

4. What is your initial response to the Lord saying, "You are mine; you are alive in Me; you reign with Me"? Does this contradict anything you have believed about yourself?

5. Does the story of the woman with the blood issue inspire you? Do you find that going after Jesus's healing is a struggle for you? What do you think prevents you from believing you are God's beloved daughter?

6. How do you think your peace in Christ (or lack of peace in Christ) correlates to your identity in Him?

7. Do you believe God sees you and responds to your individual needs and desires (see *Christ's Victory* chart on page 21)? When has He been faithful? How has His love for you changed you?

DIGGING DEEPER

Below are some recommended questions and activities to use in your personal devotion time this week.

1. **Review** the group discussion questions (above), and record in your journal any of your answers or answers of other women in your group that were particularly meaningful to you.

2. **Review** the chart on page 21. **Pray** about when you put on masks, asking the Spirit to reveal the lies you believe about these masks and your true identity.

3. **Read** Luke 23:26–24:53, **reflecting** on all that Jesus did to accomplish victory over sin, evil, and death, and how His victory established your identity.

4. **Read** Luke 8:40–56, which includes the healing of the bleeding woman as well as the raising of a dead girl. **Reflect** on His deep compassion and try to imagine how the people who were healed (as well as their loved ones) would have felt.

5. **Ask the Lord** to help you see yourself from His eyes sometime this week, and receive what it is He is offering through this revelation. **Thank Him** for revealing His truth.

6. **Listen** to one of your favorite praise songs and practice resting in His presence.

7. **"Set the Seen"** by choosing to do an activity from Appendix 1. Record in your journal what the Holy Spirit reveals and how you feel knowing you are seen by God.

Christ's Victory

"And Jesus came and said to them, 'All authority in heaven and on earth has been given to me.'" (Matthew 28:18, ESV)

Through Jesus' victory over sin and death, every human desire has been satisfied. We no longer need to put on the masks of people-pleasing, perfectionism, and performance.

Desire	Christ's Victory	What it means for the believer
To belong, be loved, and be included	Death on a cross	Sin forgiven Charges erased Claim of enemy cancelled Transferred to Jesus' Kingdom (Colossians 1 and 2)
		JESUS SAYS: "SHE IS MINE!"
To feel worthy and valuable	Resurrection	Given a new nature Given Christ's power through the Holy Spirit Given Christ's righteousness (2 Cor. 5:17-21, Romans 8)
		JESUS SAYS: "SHE IS ALIVE IN ME!"
To have purpose and significance	Ascension	Given authority with Christ Seated in the heavenly realm (Ephesians 2:4-7)
		JESUS SAYS: "SHE REIGNS WITH ME!"

SESSION 4

SEEN:

Unstuck

SMALL-GROUP DISCUSSION

1. If you completed any of the “Digging Deeper” exercises during the week and you feel comfortable sharing, explain what you learned or experienced.

2. Review John 5:1–17. Does it comfort you or disturb you that because of His compassion for people, Jesus changes direction from doing what the Law tells Him He is to do? Where else do you see Him do this in Scripture? What do you think He was trying to tell His followers about the Law and His love?

3. Read Proverbs 18:14. Have you ever had a “crushed spirit”? What difference did Jesus and God’s Word make to you during that time?

4. What do you think a person needs to surrender to Jesus for Him to heal them? What does He give in exchange?

5. If you struggle to experience true freedom, do you think you more often settle for less than what Jesus offers, or do you think you struggle because of fear? How have you seen this in your life?

6. Jesus asks questions, not because He needs answers, but because He wants connection. What question might He ask you today if He wanted you to "get up" off the mat that is keeping you down?

7. How have you heard God's voice in the past? What difference did that make in your life?

DIGGING DEEPER

Below are some recommended questions and activities to use in your personal devotion time this week.

1. **Review** the group discussion questions (above), and record in your journal any of your answers or answers of other women in your group that were particularly meaningful to you.

2. **Pray** about areas where you feel stuck right now, and ask the Lord to show you how you might be settling for less than He has for you or fearing where He might lead you. Let Him speak to your heart about this.

3. **Read** John 5:1–8 and **reflect** on Jesus's response to the invalid as if you were him. Now read verses 9–17 and reflect on Jesus's response to the religious men as if you were one of them. What differences do you see in how they might respond?

4. **Read** Acts 3:1–10 and **reflect** on how Peter and John are fulfilling Jesus's mission in this passage. **Pray** about how you might be used to bring His kingdom into your circles of influence.

5. **Ask the Lord** to reveal to you places in your life where He's helped you get unstuck, and **thank Him** for His grace.

6. **Listen** to one of your favorite praise songs and practice resting in His presence.

7. **"Set the Seen"** by choosing to do an activity from Appendix 1. Record in your journal what the Holy Spirit reveals and how you feel knowing you are seen by God.

SESSION 5

SEEN:

Unashamed

SMALL-GROUP DISCUSSION

1. If you completed any of the "Digging Deeper" exercises during the week and you feel comfortable sharing, explain what you learned or experienced.

2. Do you think you are "mindful of the devil's schemes"? In what ways are you mindful and in what ways, if any, do you regularly fall for his schemes?

3. Do you see the difference between feeling convicted over something you have done and being ashamed of who you are? Why do you think the first humans were naked and unashamed in the Garden of Eden?

4. Have you ever experienced sudden, supernatural forgiveness for someone? Why do you think the Holy Spirit moves in that way and other times forgiveness is a journey?

5. Lynne's story of praying around the lake where she was abused led her to a deeper level of healing through the revelation of truth and compassion for her abuser. Can you identify anything that she did to receive that deeper healing?

6. Where in your life have you experienced for yourself God's truth? Did you feel like it set you free? Describe that time for your group.

DIGGING DEEPER

Below are some recommended questions and activities to use in your personal devotion time this week.

1. **Review** the group discussion questions (above), and record in your journal any of your answers or answers of other women in your group that were particularly meaningful to you.

2. **Pray** about Lynne's story and why the Lord orchestrated the day the way He did for her to find freedom from her past. **Ask** the Lord to orchestrate an event in your life that's so deeply personal that there can be no doubt that you are seen by Him!

3. **Read** Genesis 2–3, and **reflect** on the shame Adam and Eve experienced, how they reacted, and what God did to cover their shame.

4. **Read** Deuteronomy 29:29. **Imagine** how God's secret revelations can positively affect future generations.

5. **Ask the Lord** to show you how you have been affected by shame in your life and how you can receive the truth that Jesus, for the joy set before Him, "...endured the cross, scorning its shame, and sat down at the right hand of the throne of God" (Hebrews 12:2b). **Thank Him** for this great sacrifice.

6. **Listen** to one of your favorite praise songs and practice resting in His presence.

7. **"Set the Seen"** by choosing to do an activity from Appendix 1. Record in your journal what the Holy Spirit reveals and how you feel knowing you are seen by God.

SESSION 6

SEEN:

Overcoming Obstacles

SMALL-GROUP DISCUSSION

1. If you completed any of the "Digging Deeper" exercises during the week and you feel comfortable sharing, explain what you learned or experienced.

2. Did Psalm 139 being read over you affect you in a new way? What stood out to you? Was there any truth that was hard for you to receive?

3. Has God delivered you from fear in any area of your life? How did that happen? What fears drive your decisions today? What could you do this week as a step of faith to overcome the obstacle?

4. Read Luke 23:32–34. Why do you think Jesus speaks about forgiving others so often? Have you seen how unforgiveness in yourself or in others can "define who you are"?

5. Is there someone you are having trouble forgiving? Do you understand why you can't forgive? Would you like the group to pray with you about that?

6. Review *Living as His Beloved Daughter* chart (on page 35), and identify some areas where you'd like to see change in your life. Take a few minutes, pair up, and pray for each other that God would move your heart to help you see yourself as Father God's beloved daughter.

7. What do you see as an action step you can take this week to start the transformation from living in the orphan realm of bondage to living freely as a child of God?

DIGGING DEEPER

Below are some recommended questions and activities to use in your personal devotion time this week.

1. **Review** the group discussion questions (above), and record in your journal any of your answers or answers of other women in your group that were particularly meaningful to you.

2. **Pray** about forgiving anyone who has harmed you. **Reflect** on all that God has forgiven you for, and ask the Lord to give you a willingness to forgive that person.

3. **Read** 1 Corinthians 13, and **reflect** on what true love is like according to God. Ask the Holy Spirit to highlight areas in your life where you are not receiving God's love or giving God's love to others.

4. **Read** Luke 22:47-51, and **reflect** on how Jesus didn't retaliate against His enemies but offered His healing instead. **Ask** the Lord how you can offer healing and holiness to others through forgiveness.

5. **Review** *Living as His Beloved Daughter* chart (on page 35). **Ask the Lord** to show you where you are living in the orphan spirit realm. Allow Him to move in whatever way He needs to bring you freedom as His daughter and **thank Him** that you are His beloved.

6. **Listen** to one of your favorite praise songs and practice resting in His presence.

7. **"Set the Seen"** by choosing to do an activity from Appendix 1. Record in your journal what the Holy Spirit reveals and how you feel knowing you are seen by God.

Living as His Beloved Daughter

"I have come that they may have life, and have it to the full."
(John 10:10)

Although each woman who trusts in Jesus as their Savior is a true daughter of God, we may not be living as one. Use this chart to help identify and pray into those areas where you are not living in your full inheritance as His beloved daughter.

Spiritual Issue	The Heart of an Orphan (Bondage)	The Heart of a Daughter (Freedom)
My relationship to God	God is Master; I am His slave	God is my loving Father; I am His beloved daughter
My perception of God's presence	Conditional and distant	Close and intimate
My dependency	Independent/self-reliant	Acknowledge my ongoing need for God
My theology	Live by the Law/legalism	Live from a place of unconditional love
My need for approval	Strive for applause of others	Accepted by grace
The reason I serve	To impress and satisfy God or others	Serve from a place of gratitude, freely and without agenda
The reason I practice spiritual disciplines	Duty/earning God's favor	Enjoy growing in my intimacy with God
My belief about purity	Must be holy to have God's favor	Want to be as close to God and as much like God as possible
How I see myself	Compare myself to others	See my value as God sees me
Where I find comfort	From things of this world: busyness, religious activity, vices	Seek times of quietness and solitude to rest in God's presence
How I relate to others	Competition, rivalry, jealousy	Humility and unity, rejoice in others' successes
How I handle other people's faults	Accusation, exposure	Seek to restore others in a spirit of love and gentleness
My view of authority	Source of pain; lack heart of submission	Respectful, honoring; see leaders as positioned by God
How I accept criticism	Blame, criticize in return, reject	Receive it humbly; view it as an opportunity to grow in Christ
How I see my future	Fight for what you can get!	As a glorious inheritance!

SESSION 7
SEEN:
Beloved

SMALL-GROUP DISCUSSION

1. If you completed any of the "Digging Deeper" exercises during the week and you feel comfortable sharing, explain what you learned or experienced.

2. Has your idea about God's love changed over the course of your life? Why do you think it changed?

3. Is there anything in your life that you have trouble believing you are forgiven for? Do you think the reason you have trouble is because you think you are not good enough, or God is not gracious enough, or something else?

4. Why do you think Jesus asks Peter, "Do you love Me?" so many times? How would you answer this question today if Jesus asked you? Could you describe what it means to love Jesus?

5. Think about Peter's life, then take 5 minutes to skim through the Book of Acts. How was his life transformed after he received the restoration from Jesus? How did others benefit from the redemption of his story?

6. Read Romans 8:28. How have you understood this verse in the past? Is the idea that we "co-create and co-labor with Jesus to bring God's beauty and goodness to the world" a new idea for you?

7. Let's dream a little. Can you imagine any way—even if it seems out of reach right now—for the Lord to redeem your story in such a way that generations are changed because of it?

DIGGING DEEPER

Below are some recommended questions and activities to use in your personal devotion time this week.

1. **Review** the group discussion questions (above), and record in your journal any of your answers or answers of other women in your group that were particularly meaningful to you.

2. **Pray** and ask the Lord to reveal any area of your life where you are not accepting that you are His beloved. Continue to listen to how He might be responding to reassure you in this area.

3. **Read** all of John 21, and **reflect** on the reasons Jesus orchestrated this scene. Pretend that you are Peter, and feel every emotion he felt, including the deep love and unconditional grace of the Lord.

4. **Read** the calling of Peter in John 1:35–42, and **reflect** on the first impressions Peter might have had of Jesus and how those might have changed during his three years with Him.

5. **Ask the Lord** to give you memories of your spiritual journey and the first impressions you might have had about God. **Thank Him** for all of the truths He's revealed to you about Himself.

6. **Listen** to one of your favorite praise songs and practice resting in His presence.

7. **"Set the Seen"** by choosing to do an activity from Appendix 1. Record in your journal what the Holy Spirit reveals and how you feel knowing you are seen by God.

SESSION 8
SEEN:
Your Best Story

SMALL-GROUP DISCUSSION

1. If you completed any of the "Digging Deeper" exercises during the week and you feel comfortable sharing, explain what you learned or experienced.

2. When was the last time you gave yourself grace to fail? How did that make you feel? Why do you think we all have such a hard time receiving God's grace?

3. After going through this Bible study, what part do you think a person plays in the redemption of their stories? What part does God play? What part do others play?

4. Lynne said, "If God had simply removed your pain, it would not be as impressive or as useful as pain redeemed." Do you think this is true? Why, or why not?

5. How has the way you view your story changed since beginning this study? Do you feel like you are now hopeful about your best story, the one that will be rewritten by God?

6. Are you feeling led to do anything different in your life so that others can benefit from the redemption of your "thorny thread"? How might that have an impact on God's Kingdom?

7. Without a doubt, the Lord led you to this study so that you can become more aware of the deep love He has for the "unmasked" you. In what ways have you been able to become more of your true self because of your participation in this small group study?

DIGGING DEEPER

Below are some recommended questions and activities to use in your personal devotion time this week.

1. **Review** the group discussion questions (above), and record in your journal any of your answers or answers of other women in your group that were particularly meaningful to you.

2. **Pray** about how you might use your redeemed story to affect the world and bring God's Kingdom. Allow the Lord to speak to you about the possibilities!

3. **Read** Psalm 107 in its entirety, and **reflect** on all of what God has done to bring deliverance and redemption in your life.

4. **Read** John 17, and **reflect** on what Jesus prayed to His Father about the unity of believers and the joy that unity brings. Ask God to reveal to you what your part of bringing unity and joy to the world looks like.

5. **Ask the Lord** to remind you of a redeemed story in your life, and **thank Him** for what He alone has done to bring it full circle.

6. **Listen** to one of your favorite praise songs and practice resting in His presence.

7. **"Set the Seen"** by choosing to do an activity from Appendix 1. Record in your journal what the Holy Spirit reveals and how you feel knowing you are seen by God.

APPENDIX 1

"Setting the Seen"
10 Intentional Ways to Experience Being Seen by God

"He will call on me, and I will answer him."
Psalm 91:15a

Our God loves to show us that He sees each of us and delights in what He sees. Sometimes we need to intentionally put ourselves in places so that we can receive.

Before you begin any of the suggestions below, pray that He will show Himself in new and powerful ways, and then set your expectations to match His promise to faithfully answer when we call.

1. Take a Silent Retreat

   Set aside 24-48 hours (or longer if you can) to retreat with the Lord in silence. It's amazing what you (with a Bible, a journal, and maybe some worship music) can experience with the Lord when you quiet your soul and seek Him.

2. Practice Visio Divina (Divine Seeing) or Lectio Divina (Divine Reading)

   These ancient practices are forms of prayer that help set your mind on the Almighty as you allow Him to speak to your heart. You can use any art or visual stimuli to mediate on things of the Lord (for Visio), or you can meditate on Scripture verses or passages (for Lectio).

3. Book a Healing Prayer Session
   Through guided healing prayer, others pray to lead you to hear from God. Search churches in your area to see if any of them offer such prayer sessions.

4. Join a Small Group
   True healing is found in communities that are safe spaces. Other Godly women who are compassionate and understanding are very beneficial in our growth to becoming our true selves.

5. Recount Being Seen
   Spend one morning each month reflecting on when and how over the last 30 days you have felt really seen by the Lord. Praise and gratefulness should be a natural response!

6. Get Out In Nature
   Find an outdoor place that you enjoy or explore a new area that you have never been before. Find Him and His beauty in the world around you. You may be surprised at how He chooses to make Himself known.

7. Be Creative
   Creativity is a divine character trait that we are each given as we reflect the image of our heavenly Creator. Our lives get busy, and we forget that we have this creative side that needs to be expressed. One idea is to get a coloring book and some nice, sharp colored pencils, and listen to praise music while you doodle and listen for His still, small voice.

8. Find a Spiritual Director
   Spiritual Directors help direct prayer so that a woman can hear from God more easily. Many famous writers and speakers have Spiritual Directors that help them get "unstuck" and bring clarity to their prayer.

9. Practice the Prophetic

    Prophetic words are powerful ways to share with others what you are hearing from the Spirit. Not only will the person you have a word for be encouraged, but you get to be the messenger and share in the sacred space!

10. Embrace Divine Appointments

    When God puts people in your path—especially if you would never dream they would be there—pay close attention to why He would orchestrate such an event. Ask Him, and respond in obedience if He is asking something from you or telling you something you need to know.

APPENDIX 2

A Letter to Group Leaders

Dear Faithful Leader,

As the leader of this small group, you have been called by God and equipped to facilitate and shepherd through the power and guidance of the Holy Spirit. You do not need to be perfect to be used in this way (or any way!); just remember *you are blessed to be a blessing*! It's been my experience that, ironically, I am the one who receives the greatest benefits by simply being willing to serve.

To help you in this endeavor, I have put together some basic guidelines for leading your small group:

BEFORE THE MEETINGS

Prepare by Reaching Out

- Contact each woman individually before the first gathering, giving her details about the time and location. Suggest that she brings her Bible, her journal, and a pen to each of the meetings, and ask her if there is anything she would like prayer for.

Prepare by Praying

- Leading up to the first meeting and continuing throughout the study, pray for any personal requests.
- Pray continuously that the women's hearts would be open to what the Lord has for them personally through this study. Ask God for each of them to experience God's love and freedom in fresh, new ways.
- Pray for the Holy Spirit to knit the group together through vulnerability and transparency. Pray that the

enemy would not have an opportunity to establish a foothold through the group dynamics.

- Pray that the Lord would guide you (and any co-leader) in ministering to the women in their journey toward wholeness and give you supernatural wisdom in shepherding them and facilitating the discussion each week.

Prepare by Setting the Room

- Set the room up with chairs that can be moved from viewing the video on the television or laptop to a circle for discussion.
- SNACKS! Ask for a volunteer each week to bring a food snack, and encourage each woman to bring the beverage of her choice each week.

AT THE MEETINGS

(Timing based on a 1½ hour meeting with one facilitator)*

Opening (20 MINUTES)

- Allow the women to mingle and get comfortable.
- Welcome everyone personally, and let them know you are glad they are there.
- Pray a brief prayer over your time together.

Teaching (20 MINUTES)

- Start the session video promptly 20 minutes after the meeting begins in order to allow adequate time for discussion (which is usually everyone's favorite part!)

Facilitate the Discussion (45 MINUTES)

- Read each question and any Scripture references. Be sure to allow enough time for each question to be answered thoroughly. Remember, you are not here to *teach*, but to facilitate the discussion and to move the women through the study questions.

- As participants begin a study, they are often reserved in sharing. The ladies should be *encouraged* to answer the questions, but never coerced or forced. Do not call on anyone, but allow the Spirit's prompting to move people to deep sharing. Always affirm the women who answer questions, even if you feel the answers are not "right".
- Some people may be embarrassed or uncomfortable hearing honest, painful stories, and they may unknowingly say something or react in a way that causes the sharing person to shut down or stop coming to the group. If someone is vulnerable, immediately recognize and validate her and her courage for sharing her story.
- Try to get through all of the questions, but do not interrupt a discussion that is flowing well in order to do so. If you don't finish a question, mark it to come back to another week if you have extra time.
- Don't be afraid of silence and don't try to fill the space. While you don't want to let the silence hang out there too long, the sacred space of the quiet is where many women learn to hear from the Lord and find their own voice.
- Although some of the questions may elicit deep emotions in some women, trust the work He is doing. The Lord will use these moments to bring breakthrough for the individual and a closeness to the group.
- Have fun! Enjoy the new friendships and the things you are learning as a leader and participant.

Closing (5 MINUTES)

- Read the Digging Deeper Questions for the session out loud, and encourage the women to pick an optional activity that will challenge them and build on the topics that were discussed in today's session. Remind them that they will be given the option to share what they discover in their Digging Deeper the following week.
- Ask participants to send you prayer requests that you can forward to the group to pray during the week.
- End in a brief prayer.

Precious Leader, thank you again for your willingness to serve the women in your community in this important way. I pray that during these next eight weeks, you will sense His presence and power flowing through and from you!

You are Seen,
Lynne

*For large groups, consider either expanding the time or breaking the group into two with two leaders instead of one.

THY NAME
thy-name.com
PUBLISHING

Made in the USA
Coppell, TX
25 April 2026

Are you longing to be truly seen?

You and I enter this world with a divine desire to be seen as our true self. Yet somewhere along the way, most of us struggle to live out our God-given identity and masks become our protection. As a result, we often end up with shallow or difficult relationships where we can't be real with anyone, even with God.

Is this the way we are supposed to live? How would our stories change if we could shed these cover-ups, discover the beauty of vulnerability, and begin to live in freedom from pretense through our relationship with Jesus?

Through eight inspiring video sessions, engaging group questions, and daily personal reflection, Lynne takes you on a guided journey of being truly seen, empowering you to break free from the façade, and step into the fullness of who God created you to be.

Lynne Farrell is a speaker, Bible study teacher, and author of the children's book, "Bennie's Forever Gift". Her ministry, Seen and Beloved, exists to help bring women into the freedom and flourishing that is only found in Jesus. Lynne lives in Arlington, Virginia with her husband, Paul. They have two adult children.

Visit www.seenandbeloved for more information.

THY NAME Publishing
www.thy-name.com

ISBN 978-1-7368128-9-1